WORDS OF CHANGE

ANTI-RACISM

WORDS
OF CHANGE

ANTI-
RACISM

POWERFUL VOICES,
INSPIRING IDEAS

KENRYA RANKIN

SPRUCE BOOKS
A Sasquatch Books Imprint

FOR SAA RANKIN NAASEL.
MAY YOU ALWAYS
CREATE IN YOUR TRUTH.

"Our people deserve the world we envision, and that world requires us to birth and build it."

—ASH-LEE WOODARD HENDERSON

INTRODUCTION

Imagine a massive ladder. It is made of solid, gray concrete. Its feet are buried deep, anchored in the earth, rooted, and it's propped up so that it stretches toward the sky.

Perched at the very top, his head impinging on the clouds, his eyes trained on the horizon, is a man. A White, middle-aged, wealthy, cisgender, heterosexual, Christian, able-bodied, citizen of a Western democracy. He stands firm, securely planted on the top rung.

Below him, stands a woman. A White, middle-aged, wealthy, cisgender, heterosexual, Christian, able-bodied, citizen of a Western democracy. Firm, secure.

On each rung below her stands someone whose identity—their race, their age, their gender expression—is met with systemic discrimination and inequity. Things get more and more precarious as you move your eyes down the ladder and notice that each of the occupants has more trouble heaped on their shoulders than the last. Weighty and unwieldy, those oppressive burdens bend them toward the earth, making it difficult to stand firm, secure.

Now imagine that the ladder, and everyone on it, is enveloped in a thick, murky, noxious smog. It makes their nostrils quiver, and they cough with each intake of air. It dulls the brilliant colors of the landscape, burns their eyes, and makes it impossible to take a deep, free breath.

That ladder is White supremacy: a political, social, and economic system that thrives on the subjugation of people who have not been let into Whiteness. It's bolstered by racism, classism, homophobia, ageism, ableism, nativism, transphobia, sexism, and more. And that smog? That's also White supremacy (that showoff is literally everywhere). While the folks up top think they're doing well—and they are, relatively—they are still being slowly poisoned by the same toxic system that fells everyone who has been slotted in below them.

Your place in this system dictates everything: the water you drink, the schools you attend, how much money your family has, your safety, your life expectancy. Where are you on the ladder? Does your identity put you at the top, where the air is a teensy bit clearer and the view is a hell of a lot better? Or have you been pushed to the bottom, where you are forced to live in a toxic environment?

While it can sometimes be difficult to see it, you likely enjoy privilege that someone else doesn't have. Perhaps you identify as the gender you were assigned at birth—congratulations, you have privilege over our trans family. Or maybe you have the full, unfettered use of your body; you have opportunities that our folks of color who are living with disabilities on the rung below you don't enjoy. School and work are important, but our real job is to use that privilege, however invisible it may seem on the worst days, to bring down the hierarchy.

This beautiful book is here to help. As the name suggests, this book tackles racism, the sturdiest and stubbornest of the supports that prop up White supremacy. On the following pages, you will find wisdom, inspiration, and encouragement from people who are doing the work of banishing racism. Note that I didn't say the work of not being racist; this fight requires more from us than simply saying, "I love all people" or working hard not to personally engage in racist acts. It requires us, you, to actively engage, to use our privilege to advocate for all, to be staunchly anti-racist. This book will show you how.

But this book is more than just a guide—it's a celebration of the voices that shout above the madness and a chronicle of the fight we are collectively waging. It acknowledges the hard work we've done, the seemingly unsurmountable tasks we undertake each day, and the dreams we carry for the future. It is, my friends, hope.

Let's work together to clear the air and rip the ladder from the earth so that our system can never again support the weight of racism.

In solidarity,

Kenrya

I'm so inspired when I see
people who have a way that they
do things, have a way that they
think about the world, and they're
courageous enough to be open
to listening to what the experiences
are of so many of us who want to
live in world that's just and want to
live in a world that's equitable.

—ALICIA GARZA

"

WHAT WOULD AMERICA BE LIKE IF WE LOVED BLACK PEOPLE AS MUCH AS WE LOVE BLACK CULTURE?

—AMANDLA STENBERG

"

"Colorblindness, while nice
in theory, has no effect on structural
and institutional racism. Racism
is a system, and that system benefits
certain people at the expense
of others. Ignoring it just lets those
problems persist."

—FRANCHESCA RAMSEY

"This inseparable relationship between humans and the earth, inherent to Indigenous peoples, must be learned, must be embraced and respected by all people for the sake of all of our future generations and all of humanity. I urge all of you, all humanity to join with us in transforming the social structures, the institutions and power relations that underpin conditions of oppression and exploitation."

—TOM B. K. GOLDTOOTH

"IN A RACIST SOCIETY, IT'S NOT ENOUGH TO BE NON-RACIST— WE MUST BE ANTI-RACIST."

—ANGELA DAVIS

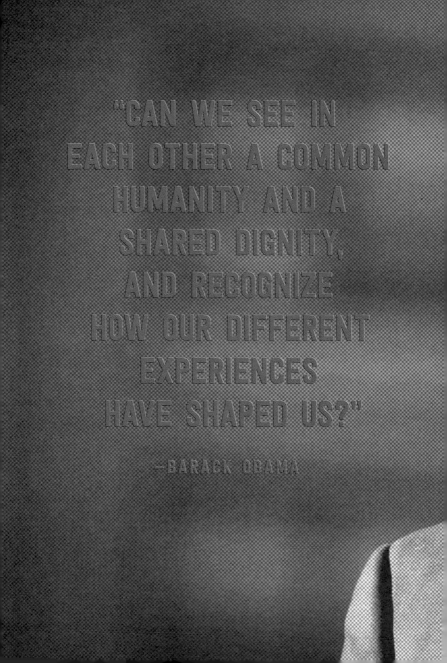

"CAN WE SEE IN EACH OTHER A COMMON HUMANITY AND A SHARED DIGNITY, AND RECOGNIZE HOW OUR DIFFERENT EXPERIENCES HAVE SHAPED US?"

—BARACK OBAMA

"INTIMACY
ALLOWS THE
TRANSFORMATION
WE SO
DESPERATELY
NEED, BEYOND
WHITENESS
AS SUPERIORITY."

—ADRIENNE MAREE BROWN

It is insufficient to only tell your children that racism and racists are bad. It is insufficient to simply explain 'we love people of all colors.' It is lazy and near damaging to proclaim a love for all people but never make the leap of actually reaching out to people of color or adding tangible diversity to your life. In a world filled with empty rhetoric, our children don't need to hear words from us without action. They need to see us embody the beliefs we claim to hold dear.

—BELLAMY SHOFFNER

"Differences are not intended
to separate, to alienate.
We are different precisely
in order to realize
our need of one another."

—ARCHBISHOP DESMOND TUTU

> WHITE SUPREMACY IS THIS NATION'S OLDEST PYRAMID SCHEME. EVEN THOSE WHO HAVE LOST EVERYTHING TO THE SCHEME ARE STILL HANGING IN THERE, WAITING FOR THEIR TURN TO CASH OUT.

—IJEOMA OLUO

There's this false notion that you have to separate and choose between issues of class and issues of race. What people do when they say that you need to separate class from race is that they are really just saying that people of color should come second. There is no such thing as talking about class without there being implications of the racial history of the United States. You just can't do it.

—ALEXANDRIA OCASIO-CORTEZ

"HISTORY MUST RESTORE WHAT SLAVERY TOOK AWAY, FOR IT IS THE SOCIAL DAMAGE OF SLAVERY THAT THE PRESENT GENERATION MUST REPAIR AND OFFSET."

—ARTURO ALFONSO SCHOMBURG

An anti-racist person is on a
life-long journey that includes
forming new understanding
of and ways to live her or his racial
identity and then increasing
commitment to and engagement
in anti-racism actions.

—LOUISE DERMAN-SPARKS
& PATRICIA G. RAMSEY

INTERGENERATIONAL LEADERSHIP IS THE LIFELINE AND THREAD THROUGH WHICH WE CAN MOVE OUR MOVEMENT FOR PEACE, LOVE, AND LIBERATION.

—BECKIE MASAKI

"No one becomes 'not racist,'
despite a tendency by Americans to
identify themselves that way.
We can only strive to be 'anti-racist'
on a daily basis, to continually
rededicate ourselves to the lifelong
task of overcoming our country's
racist heritage."

—IBRAM X. KENDI

OUR FUTURE SURVIVAL IS PREDICATED UPON OUR ABILITY TO RELATE WITHIN EQUALITY.

—AUDRE LORDE

"Our collective stories of race in the US are not easy to own. They are stories of slavery, violence, and systemic dehumanization. We will have to choose courage over comfort. We will have to feel our way through the shame and sorrow. We will have to listen. We will have to challenge our resistance and our defensiveness. We have to keep listening even when we want to scream, 'I'm not that way. This isn't my fault!'"

—BRENÉ BROWN

WHAT WE NEED NOW
MORE THAN EVER
IS A HUMAN RIGHTS
MOVEMENT THAT
CHALLENGES SYSTEMIC
RACISM IN EVERY
SINGLE CONTEXT.

—OPAL TOMETI

"

IF YOU STICK A KNIFE
IN MY BACK NINE
INCHES AND PULL
IT OUT SIX INCHES,
THERE'S NO PROGRESS.
IF YOU PULL IT ALL THE
WAY OUT, THAT'S NOT
PROGRESS. PROGRESS
IS HEALING THE WOUND
THAT THE BLOW MADE.

—MALCOLM X

"

THE CAUSE OF
FREEDOM IS NOT
THE CAUSE OF A RACE
OR A SECT, A PARTY
OR A CLASS—IT IS THE
CAUSE OF HUMANKIND,
THE VERY BIRTHRIGHT
OF HUMANITY.

—ANNA JULIA COOPER

"AT THE INTERSECTION
OF OPPRESSION AND
RESISTANCE LIES THE
RADICAL POTENTIAL
OF QUEERNESS TO
CHALLENGE AND BRING
TOGETHER ALL THOSE
DEEMED MARGINAL AND
ALL THOSE COMMITTED
TO LIBERATORY POLITICS."

—CATHY J. COHEN

I want to love and rage, mourn and
struggle, with millions of others,
against this killing machine, until
we shut it down for good—replacing
it with social goodness that we can
barely yet envision, and armed with
do-it-ourselves, steel-hard solidarity
as shield, aid, humanity, ethic.

—CINDY MILSTEIN

"WE ALLOW EACH OTHER SO LITTLE ENJOYMENT OR EVEN TOLERANCE FOR OUR INDIVIDUALITIES, OUR UNIQUENESSES, AND YET TO ME, THAT'S WHAT IT'S ALL ABOUT."

—BUFFY SAINTE-MARIE

SOME PEOPLE SAY YOU
FIGHT FIRE BEST WITH
FIRE, BUT WE SAY YOU
PUT FIRE OUT BEST
WITH WATER. WE SAY
YOU DON'T FIGHT RACISM
WITH RACISM. WE'RE
GONNA FIGHT RACISM
WITH SOLIDARITY.

—FRED HAMPTON

"You cannot expect something
to happen without your
doing something, without taking
action. If you want something
done, then you have to organize
something around it."

—DENNIS BANKS

WE WHO BELIEVE IN FREEDOM CANNOT REST.

—ELLA BAKER

"Creeping Whiteness inevitably means that some people of color will be invited to join the White category, with the promise of attaining the privileges of Whiteness. South Asians, Arabs, and other Asians have historically been tempted to take this racial bribe in order to advance to higher positions on the racial hierarchy. We must firmly decline this invitation. When we do so, we can begin to dismantle the racial ladder altogether."

—DEEPA IYER

Hate is not inborn;
it has to be constantly cultivated,
to be brought into being,
in conflict with more or less
recognized guilt complexes.
Hate demands existence and
he who hates has to show
his hate in appropriate actions
and behavior; in a sense,
he has to become hate.

—FRANTZ FANON

THE WAY TO RIGHT WRONGS IS TO TURN THE LIGHT OF TRUTH UPON THEM.

—IDA B. WELLS

WE HAVE SUCH A STRONG DESIRE TO LIVE WITH HOPE AND HUMAN DIGNITY THAT EXISTENCE WITHOUT THEM IS IMPOSSIBLE.

—HUEY P. NEWTON

"Treating different things the same can generate as much inequality as treating the same things differently."

—KIMBERLÉ CRENSHAW

Once social change begins
it cannot be reversed.
You cannot uneducate the
person who has learned
to read. You cannot
humiliate the person who
feels pride. You cannot
oppress the people who are
not afraid anymore.

—CÉSAR CHÁVEZ

"WE ARE ALL ONE
AND IF WE
DON'T KNOW,
WE WILL LEARN IT
THE HARD WAY."

—BAYARD RUSTIN

"We don't have to reinvent the idea of multiracial, multicultural unity. It's been done before. If we can break through the divisive presentation of history that makes it look like none of our communities came together, all we need to do is look at real history, and see that it's been done before. We've stood up together before and we accomplished things and made a difference for all people and all human beings."

—HELEN ZIA

RACISM IS FUNDAMENTALLY A FEMINIST ISSUE BECAUSE IT IS SO INTERCONNECTED WITH SEXIST OPPRESSION.

−BELL HOOKS

FRIENDLY REMINDER THAT YOU DON'T HAVE TO SAY THE 'N-WORD' TO BE RACIST. THAT'S NOT THE SOLE REQUIREMENT. ASKING PEOPLE TO PROVE RACISM IS ANOTHER TOOL THE OPPRESSOR USES TO MARGINALIZE AND DISCREDIT US.

—LIZZO

I AM HOPEFUL BECAUSE I HAVE FAITH IN BLACK LIBERATION, WHICH IS TO SAY, THE FREEDOM WE DREAM AND PRACTICE WHEN WE REFUSE TO SET FIRE TO ANOTHER'S POTENTIAL TO LOVE, TO LAUGH, TO LIVE.

—DARNELL MOORE

"I'm always struck by how often people act as though racial differentiation is natural. . . . I don't think that's natural, actually. I think the natural condition is for human beings to actually have the capacity to identify and resonate with one another. I think the creation of Whiteness actually does something to close off."

—IMANI PERRY

THEY TELL ME BLACK BODIES ARE WORTHLESS; I TELL THEM THIS BLACK BODY IS SACRED.

—HAYLIN BELAY

Each and every one of us has the capacity to be an oppressor. I want to encourage each and every one of us to interrogate how we might be an oppressor and how we might be able to become liberators for ourselves and for each other.

—LAVERNE COX

"MY STRUGGLE HAS
MADE ME FIERCE, AND
WE ALL NEED TO BE
A LITTLE FIERCE TO GET
THINGS DONE."

—DEB HAALAND

"Silence and inaction only serve to perpetuate the status quo of race relations. Will we, as a nation, choose the path we have always traveled, a journey of silence that has benefited only a select group and oppressed others, or will we show courage and choose the road less traveled, a journey of racial reality that may be full of discomfort and pain, but offers benefits to all groups in our society?"

—DERALD WING SUE

ANTI-RACIST,
FOR ME, IS MORE
INDICATIVE OF A
PROCESS OF COMING
TO A HEALTHY AND
FUNCTIONING SENSE
OF A WHITE
RACIAL IDENTITY.

–DIANE FLINN

"It is never too late to give
up our prejudices."

—HENRY DAVID THOREAU

"

SAYING THAT
I'M OBSESSED WITH
RACE AND RACISM
IN AMERICA IS
LIKE SAYING I'M
OBSESSED WITH
SWIMMING WHEN
I'M DROWNING.

—HARI KONDABOLU

"

PREJUDICE GOES BOTH
WAYS, YOU KNOW.
THERE ARE PEOPLE
WHO SUFFER FROM IT,
AND THERE
ARE PEOPLE WHO
PROFIT FROM IT.

—JODI PICOULT

"People who treat other people
as less than human must not be
surprised when the bread they have
cast on the waters comes floating
back to them, poisoned."

—JAMES BALDWIN

The history of racism in this
country is White history, we know
it, it is the story of our parents,
grandparents, and ourselves.
Why do we call upon those who have
suffered the injustice of
that history to explain it to us?

—ELLEN PENCE

"THE ORIGINAL CREATION OF RACIAL CATEGORIES WAS IN THE SERVICE OF OPPRESSION."

—DR. BEVERLY DANIEL TATUM

I Sell the Shadow to Support the Substance.

SOJOURNER TRUTH.

IT IS HARD FOR THE OLD SLAVEHOLDING SPIRIT TO DIE, BUT DIE IT MUST.

—SOJOURNER TRUTH

"I REALLY BELIEVE THAT ACTIVISM IS THERAPEUTIC."

–KIYOSHI KUROMIYA

Christianity has run aground
on the rocks of racism and threatens
to capsize—it has lost its integrity.
By contrast, courageous Christianity
embraces racial and ethnic
diversity. It stands against any
person, policy, or practice that
would dim the glory of God
reflected in the life of human beings
from every tribe and tongue.

—JEMAR TISBY

We need to raise the bar, elevate
our standards for racial literacy.
Because without investing in an
education that values both the
stories and statistics, the people and
the numbers, the interpersonal
and the systemic, there will always
be a piece missing.

—WINONA GUO & PRIYA VULCHI

"AS CAUCASIAN PEOPLE, IT'S OUR JOB, IT'S OUR TASK, IT'S OUR RESPONSIBILITY TO SPEAK UP IN EVERY SINGLE ROOM WE WALK INTO. IT'S OUR JOB BECAUSE WE CREATED THE PROBLEM."

—ELLEN POMPEO

WE ARE ALL
IMPLICATED WHEN WE
ALLOW OTHER PEOPLE
TO BE MISTREATED.
AN ABSENCE OF
COMPASSION CAN
CORRUPT THE DECENCY
OF A COMMUNITY,
A STATE, A NATION.

—BRYAN STEVENSON

"I stand on the shoulders
of a generation of
young people of color that
are united, that clearly
understand that we are
suffering from structural
racism, institutional
racism, and capitalism.
We are fighting for survival."

—ROSA CLEMENTE

NOW IS THE TIME
FOR WHITE PEOPLE OF
CONSCIENCE TO ACT—
IT IS TIME TO DIG IN,
IT IS TIME TO BE BOLD,
AND IT IS TIME TO
START MAKING UP FOR
CENTURIES OF
LOST TIME.

—ERIN HEANEY & HEATHER CRONK

IT CAN BE
DAUNTING,
EXHAUSTING,
AND INTIMIDATING
AT TIMES,
BUT NEVER STOP
PUSHING FOR
CHANGE.

—ELAINE WELTEROTH

If there is no struggle there is no progress. Those who profess to favor freedom and yet depreciate agitation, are men who want crops without plowing up the ground, they want rain without thunder and lightning. They want the ocean without the awful roar of its many waters.

This struggle may be a moral one; or it may be a physical one; or it may be both moral and physical; but it must be a struggle. Power concedes nothing without a demand. It never did and it never will.

—FREDERICK DOUGLASS

Conly   Boston

"IF I RULED THE WORLD, I WOULD FREE BLACK PEOPLE FROM EVER HAVING TO THINK ABOUT WHITE PEOPLE IN A WAY THAT CENTERS THEM."

—MICHAEL ARCENEAUX

The way forward requires a White America that strives to collaborate rather than dominate, with a mind-set of openness and interconnectedness that we have all-too-frequently neglected.

—JONATHAN METZL

"THE MORE I'VE BEEN ABLE TO LEARN ABOUT GAY RIGHTS AND EQUAL PAY AND GENDER EQUITY AND RACIAL INEQUALITY, THE MORE THAT IT ALL INTERSECTS. YOU CAN'T REALLY PICK IT APART. IT'S ALL INTERTWINED. GOD FORBID YOU BE A GAY WOMAN AND A PERSON OF COLOR IN THIS COUNTRY, BECAUSE YOU'D BE REALLY FUCKED."

—MEGAN RAPINOE

THE ONLY WAY TO SURVIVE IS BY TAKING CARE OF ONE ANOTHER.

—GRACE LEE BOGGS

"If you're seeing your White counterparts engage in White privilege behind closed doors and engaging in racism, it's your job as a White person to use your White privilege to let them know why that's so fucked up."

—JONATHAN VAN NESS

"YOU LOSE
A LOT OF TIME
HATING PEOPLE."

—MARIAN ANDERSON

White people,
White men, need to be
more outraged with
the injustices of racism
and discrimination
than we are when someone
is telling us that they
don't like something that
we are doing.

—MATT McGORRY

RACISM IS A HEART
DISEASE. HOW WE
THINK AND RESPOND IS
AT THE CORE OF RACIAL
SUFFERING AND RACIAL
HEALING. IF WE CANNOT
THINK CLEARLY AND
RESPOND WISELY, WE WILL
CONTINUE TO DAMAGE
THE WORLD'S HEART.

—RUTH KING

We are constantly being told
that we don't have racism in this
country anymore, but most of
the people who are saying that are
White. White people think
it isn't happening because it isn't
happening to them.

—JANE ELLIOTT

"THE MOST PRESENT
DAILY MANIFESTATION
OF OUR WHITE
PRIVILEGE IS THE
POSSIBILITY OF
FORGETTING ABOUT
RACISM. WE CANNOT."

—JONA OLSSON

"I LOOK AT AN ANT AND I SEE MYSELF: A NATIVE SOUTH AFRICAN, ENDOWED BY NATURE WITH A STRENGTH MUCH GREATER THAN MY SIZE SO I MIGHT COPE WITH THE WEIGHT OF A RACISM THAT CRUSHES MY SPIRIT."

—MIRIAM MAKEBA

"Some of God's people are White, some Black, some Brown, some Yellow. God didn't intend all people to be alike, not even in families. But people were intended to live in harmony, as when the strings of the ukulele blend. There is a tremendous job ahead to bring all people in tune with God. Then they will be in tune with each other."

—REV. ABRAHAM KAHIKINA AKAKA

IF YOU BELIEVE IN A CAUSE, BE WILLING TO STAND UP FOR THAT CAUSE WITH A MILLION PEOPLE OR BY YOURSELF.

—OTIS S. JOHNSON

ONE WONDERS JUST
HOW MANY TEACHING
MOMENTS WE NEED FOR
WHITE PEOPLE TO NO
LONGER FEEL ENTITLED
TO COMMENT ON OR
POLICE BLACK BODIES.

—ROXANE GAY

"Racism is man's gravest threat to man, the maximum of hatred for a minimum of reason, the maximum of cruelty for a minimum of thinking."

—RABBI ABRAHAM JOSHUA HESCHEL

"STRONG COMMUNITIES
ARE BORN OUT
OF INDIVIDUALS BEING
THEIR BEST SELVES."

—LEANNE BETASAMOSAKE SIMPSON

Time and again, White people
acting as allies in other people's
'progress' have not just failed
to address racist power relations; they
have entrenched White dominance.
Altruism cannot be the basis for
White anti-racist action. There's only
one thing that can: solidarity.

—JESSE A. MYERSON

"LIBERATION IS WHERE A DIFFERENCE IS SEEN AS AN ASSET AND NOT A LIABILITY."

—PASTOR MICHAEL McBRIDE

There is no anti-racist certification class. It's a set of socioeconomic traps and cultural values that are fired up every time we interact with the world. It is a thing you have to keep scooping out of the boat of your life to keep from drowning in it. I know it's hard work, but it's the price you pay for owning everything.

—SCOTT WOODS

IF YOU WANT PEACE, WORK FOR JUSTICE.

—POPE PAUL VI

"No one is born hating another person because of the color of his skin, or his background, or his religion. People must learn to hate, and if they can learn to hate, they can be taught to love, for love comes more naturally to the human heart than its opposite."

—NELSON MANDELA

"WE ARE NOT MYTHS
OF THE PAST,
RUINS IN THE JUNGLE,
OR ZOOS. WE ARE
PEOPLE AND WE WANT
TO BE RESPECTED,
NOT TO BE VICTIMS
OF INTOLERANCE AND
RACISM."

—RIGOBERTA MENCHÚ TUM

I don't know how to save the world. I don't have the answers or The Answer. I hold no secret knowledge as to how to fix the mistakes of generations past and present. I only know that without compassion and respect for all of earth's inhabitants, none of us will survive— nor will we deserve to.

—LEONARD PELTIER

"The dynamism of any diverse community depends not only on the diversity itself but on promoting a sense of belonging among those who formerly would have been considered and felt themselves outsiders."

—SONIA SOTOMAYOR

"

STOPPING OUR
RACIST PATTERNS
MUST BE MORE
IMPORTANT THAN
WORKING TO CONVINCE
OTHERS THAT WE
DON'T HAVE THEM.

—ROBIN DIANGELO

"

The way to lose any earthly kingdom is to be inflexible, intolerant, and prejudicial. Another way is to be too flexible, tolerant of too many wrongs, and without judgment at all. It is a razor's edge. It is the width of a blade of pili grass.

—QUEEN LILI'UOKALANI

I want to abolish the privileges
of the white skin. The White race is
like a private club based on one
huge assumption: that all those who
look White are, whatever their
complaints or reservations,
fundamentally loyal to the race.
We want to dissolve the club,
to explode it.

—NOEL IGNATIEV

"NEVER /
TRUST ANYONE /
WHO SAYS /
THEY DO NOT
SEE COLOR. /
THIS MEANS /
TO THEM, /
YOU ARE INVISIBLE."

—NAYYIRAH WAHEED

"EDUCATION SHOULD LEAD
TO INFORMED ACTION, AND
INFORMED ACTION SHOULD
LEAD TO LIBERATION,
JUSTICE, AND REPAIR."

—LECRAE

The side of history on which
we find ourselves is not determined
by whether or not we share the
experiences of one horror or
another, or how we individually
identify, but instead on our
own resolution to see the end
of each of these miseries that
perpetuate this racist, capitalist,
shit show called society.

—FINN FEINBERG

"For a few seconds, I remembered
that the most abusive parts
of our nation obsessively neglect
yesterday while peddling in
possibility. I remembered that we
got here by refusing to honestly
remember together. I remember
that it was easier to promise
than it was to reckon or change."

—KIESE LAYMON

BEING AN ACTIVIST IS NOT A SPECIAL CALLING OR A SOLITARY, COURAGEOUS OCCUPATION. WE ALL HAVE THE POTENTIAL TO BE ACTIVISTS IF WE SHOW UP, PAY ATTENTION, AND LISTEN TO EACH OTHER.

—ARIA CHIODO

IT WAS WE, THE
PEOPLE; NOT WE, THE
WHITE MALE CITIZENS;
NOR YET WE, THE
MALE CITIZENS; BUT
WE, THE WHOLE
PEOPLE, WHO FORMED
THE UNION.

—SUSAN B. ANTHONY

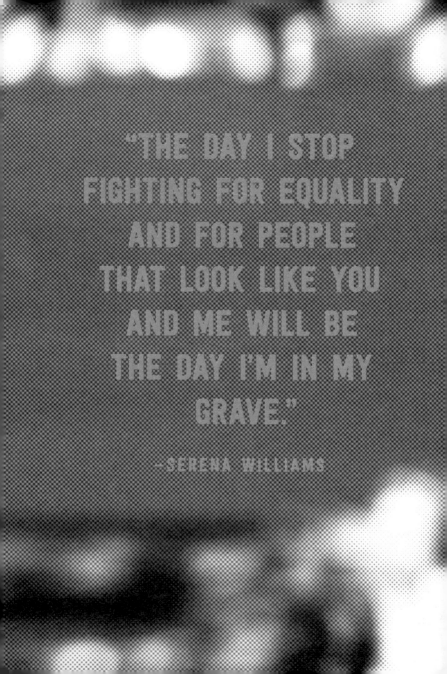
"THE DAY I STOP FIGHTING FOR EQUALITY AND FOR PEOPLE THAT LOOK LIKE YOU AND ME WILL BE THE DAY I'M IN MY GRAVE."

—SERENA WILLIAMS

Given that the US economy and political system are rooted in anti-Blackness, claiming our place in America means that we must take a position when faced with the separate but unequal worlds of Whiteness and Blackness. We are either left or right of the color line. There is no sitting that out.

—SOYA JUNG

"WE MUST ALL LEARN TO LIVE TOGETHER AS BROTHERS—OR WE WILL ALL PERISH TOGETHER AS FOOLS."

—REV. DR. MARTIN LUTHER KING JR.

Knowing and owning our ethnic narratives helps us understand the real issues of injustice, racial tension, and disunity that exist in the world. Ethnicity awareness helps us ask the question of how to prophetically engage in pursuing justice, racial reconciliation, and caring for the poor.

—SARAH SHIN

"BELIEF IN THE
HUMANITY OF BLACK
PEOPLE IS THE FIRST
TELLING BLOW TO
WHITE SUPREMACY."

—SHAWN DOVE

"

WE CAN'T THROW THE WORST PART OF RACISM INTO THE DUSTBIN OF HISTORY.

—W. KAMAU BELL

"

The thing about
anti-racism that [. . .] sits at
the core of who I am is that
I should never have to make
myself small for everyone
else to feel comfortable
about my existence. . . .
Self-actualization is at the
core of an anti-racist world.

—JASON REYNOLDS

"WHITE
SUPREMACY
IS NOT
A SHARK,
IT'S THE
WATER."

—KYLE "GUANTE" TRAN MYHRE

"White privilege is your
history being part of the core
curriculum and mine
being taught as an elective."

—OZY ALOZIEM

ONE OF THE PRIMARY
ISSUES WE MUST FACE,
ESPECIALLY IN THIS
SOCIOPOLITICAL CLIMATE,
IS THE NEED FOR
WHITE PEOPLE TO DO
THE HARD WORK OF
WRESTLING WITH WHAT
IT REALLY MEANS
TO BE WHITE.

—REV. DR. BRENDA SALTER McNEIL

SOMETIMES, I FEEL
DISCRIMINATED AGAINST,
BUT IT DOES NOT
MAKE ME ANGRY.
IT MERELY ASTONISHES
ME. HOW CAN
ANY DENY THEMSELVES
THE PLEASURE OF
MY COMPANY? IT'S
BEYOND ME.

—ZORA NEALE HURSTON

But all our phrasing—race relations, racial chasm, racial justice, racial profiling, White privilege, even White supremacy—serves to obscure that racism is a visceral experience, that it dislodges brains, blocks airways, rips muscle, extracts organs, cracks bones, breaks teeth. You must never look away from this.

—TA-NEHISI COATES

WHAT IF IN
HEAVEN WE COULD
HAVE WHITE THINGS /
AND NOT BE
WHITE HOW WOULD
WE KNOW /
HOW GOOD IT WAS
IF IT WAS GOOD FOR
EVERYONE.

—SHANE MCCRAE

OUR ULTIMATE OBJECTIVE IN LEARNING ABOUT ANYTHING IS TO TRY TO CREATE AND DEVELOP A MORE JUST SOCIETY THAN WE HAVE SEEN.

—YURI KOCHIYAMA

"We have reached an era in which the
existing system is on the verge of
collapse, with colonizer and colonized
alike resting near a precipitous edge.
We can either succumb to the ongoing
discourse of complacency propagated
by the colonizing government, or we can
mobilize for revolutionary change."

—WAZIYATAWIN

Racism will disappear when it's [. . .] no longer profitable and no longer psychologically useful. . . . If you take racism away from certain people—I mean vitriolic racism as well as the sort of social racist— if you take that away, they may have to face something really terrible—misery, self-misery, and deep pain about who they are. It's just easier to say, 'That one over there is the cause of all my problems.'

—TONI MORRISON

"

MY VOICE MUST EXIST TO ECHO RATHER THAN TO ERASE.

—ZIAD AHMED

"

"White people who truly want to be allies can find their path to ally-ship without Black validation and without us having to take time out of our days to educate them. They can find their own curriculum and figure out for themselves how they can do their part in fighting the good fight. And they can do it without the promise of Black praise."

—ZACK LINLY

BIOGRAPHIES

ZIAD AHMED *(he/him)* describes himself as an American-Muslim-Bangladeshi student activist. A speaker and entrepreneur, he runs a Generation Z consulting group and nonprofit Redefy, which aims to help organizations be more inclusive.

REV. ABRAHAM KAHIKINA AKAKA *(he/him)* was billed as Hawai'i's most widely known member of the clergy. Committed to justice, he ran the Kawaiahao Church and the The Rev. Akaka Ministries Foundation.

OZY ALOZIEM *(she/her)* is a psycho-anthropological researcher and critical Black feminist. She served as delegate to the United Nations Commission on the Status of Women in 2019, and is committed to advocating for Black lives across the diaspora.

MARIAN ANDERSON *(she/her)* was the first Black person to perform with the New York Metropolitan Opera. After the Daughters of the American Revolution organization refused to let her sing in its concert hall, she held an iconic concert at the Lincoln Memorial that later became a symbol of the Civil Rights Movement.

SUSAN B. ANTHONY *(she/her)* was a leader of the US women's suffrage movement. She traveled the nation giving speeches about the importance of abolition, temperance, and equal pay for equal work. She joined forces with Elizabeth Cady Stanton to found the American Equal Rights Association and the National Woman Suffrage Association. She later led the massive National American Woman Suffrage Association.

MICHAEL ARCENEAUX *(he/him)* is the *New York Times*-bestselling author of *I Can't Date Jesus: Love, Sex, Family, Race, and Other Reasons I've Put My Faith in Beyoncé*. An essay he wrote about how Black Twitter users impact national discourse is required reading for a course at Harvard University.

ELLA BAKER *(she/her)* was an organizer with many key organizations during the Civil Rights Movement, including the Southern Christian Leadership Conference, the National Association for the Advancement of Colored People, and the Student Nonviolent Coordinating Committee, which she helped create.

JAMES BALDWIN *(he/him)* was a writer and activist whose work centered his experience as a Black man who grew up in White America. He often attributed his clarity to the considerable time he spent living outside a country that sought to oppress him and people who looked like him.

DENNIS BANKS *(he/him)* was also known as Nowa Cumig. He was an Ojibwe and Turtle Clan activist who cofounded the American Indian Movement (AIM) and captured national attention in 1973 when he and his conspirators occupied Wounded Knee, South Dakota, the site of an 1890 massacre of Indigenous people, to bring attention to the US government's refusal to honor its treaties.

HAYLIN BELAY *(she/her)* is a sex educator and holistic health professional whose integrated mind-body-spirit practice centers reproductive justice and youth empowerment.

W. KAMAU BELL *(he/him)* is a comedian, author, and television host who tackles issues of structural racism in books like *The Awkward Thoughts of W. Kamau Bell: Tales of a 6'4", African American, Heterosexual, Cisgender, Left-Leaning, Asthmatic, Black and Proud Blerd, Mama's Boy, Dad, and Stand-Up Comedian* and shows like *United Shades of America with W. Kamau Bell*.

GRACE LEE BOGGS *(she/her)* was a social and racial activist whose work lifted up women and people of color. The child of Chinese immigrants, she joined forces with her husband, activist James Boggs, to create Detroit Summer, a community movement that united people across race, culture, and socioeconomic class to revitalize Detroit.

ADRIENNE MAREE BROWN *(she/her)* is a writer, social justice facilitator, pleasure activist, healer, and doula. Author of *Pleasure Activism: The Politics of Feeling Good* and *Emergent Strategy: Shaping Change, Changing Worlds*, she facilitates the visionary development of people, organizations, and movements.

BRENÉ BROWN *(she/her)* is a research professor at the University of Houston whose work explores courage, empathy, shame, and vulnerability. She is the author of several books, including *Daring Greatly*, *The Gifts of Imperfection*, and *Rising Strong*.

CÉSAR CHÁVEZ *(he/him)* was a labor reform organizer and civil rights activist. Born in Arizona to Mexican immigrant parents, his early years spent working on farms led him to create the National Farm Workers Association, which later became United Farm Workers. He often put his own body on the line to improve working conditions and pay for farmworkers.

ARIA CHIODO *(she/her)* is a teacher, writer and self-described "angry liberal."

ROSA CLEMENTE *(she/her)* is an organizer and independent journalist. In 2008, she became the first Afro-Latina woman to run for vice president of the United States. She and her Green Party running mate Cynthia McKinney were the only women of color ticket to run for the top spot in the history of the nation.

TA-NEHISI COATES *(he/him)* is the author of five books, including *The Water Dancer*, *We Were Eight Years in Power*, *Between the World and Me*, and Marvel Comics' *The Black Panther* and *Captain America*. He serves as a distinguished writer in residence at NYU's Arthur L. Carter Journalism Institute, is a MacArthur Fellow, and spoke before Congress about the need for reparations for Black people in America.

CATHY J. COHEN *(she/her)* is a professor of political science at The College at the University of Chicago and author of *Democracy Remixed: Black Youth and the Future of American Politics*. She created and manages the GenForward Survey and the Black Youth Project.

ANNA JULIA COOPER *(she/her)* was an educator and a scholar whose seminal work, *A Voice From the South*, chronicled the ways intersecting oppressors impact the lives of Black women. She was one of the first African American women to earn a doctoral degree.

LAVERNE COX *(she/her)* is an actress, documentary film producer, and advocate for equal rights. Her star turn on *Orange Is the New Black* made her the first trans woman of color to portray a lead character on a scripted television show. She is committed to helping people move beyond gender expectations and live more authentic lives.

KIMBERLÉ CRENSHAW *(she/her)* created the theory of intersectionality. She is professor of law at UCLA and Columbia Law School, the cofounder and executive director of think tank African American Policy Forum, and coeditor of *Critical Race Theory: Key Documents That Shaped the Movement*.

HEATHER CRONK *(she/her)* led nonprofit GetEQUAL, a LGBTQIA+ advocacy organization.

ANGELA DAVIS *(she/her)* is an activist, educator, and writer whose work explores race, criminal justice reform, and gender equality. She has been affiliated with many liberatory organizations over the years, including the Black Panther Party for Self Defense and the Che-Lumumba Club, and she is distinguished professor emerita in the humanities department at University of California, Santa Cruz.

LOUISE DERMAN-SPARKS *(she/her)* is an early childhood anti-bias educator

for both children and the adults who loom large in their lives. She cowrote *What If All the Kids Are White?: Anti-Bias Multicultural Education with Young Children and Families* with **PATRICIA G. RAMSEY**.

ROBIN DIANGELO *(she/her)* is an affiliate associate professor of education at the University of Washington, a racial justice trainer, and author of the bestseller *White Fragility: Why It's So Hard for White People to Talk About Racism*.

FREDERICK DOUGLASS *(he/him)* was born into slavery, but died a free man who used his acquired privilege and oratory skills to argue for abolition of the peculiar institution. Founder of weekly paper *The North Star*, he also wrote *Narrative of the Life of Frederick Douglass, an American Slave, Written by Himself*, and *My Bondage and My Freedom*, which challenged racial segregation.

SHAWN DOVE *(he/him)* is the founder and CEO of the Campaign for Black Male Achievement. His work centers around creating platforms to amplify the voices and stories of marginalized people and communities.

JANE ELLIOTT *(she/her)* is a White educator and diversity trainer who conducted the now famous Blue Eyes/Brown Eyes Exercise in 1968 to teach her students about racism.

FRANTZ FANON *(he/him)* was an activist and psychiatrist. Born in Martinique, he was a voice for the Algerian revolution against French colonialism. His book *Black Skin, White Masks* broke down his theories on how racism impacted Black people.

FINN FEINBERG *(he/him)* is a Bay Area anarchist.

DIANE FLINN *(she/her)* is managing partner of Diversity Matters consultancy.

ALICIA GARZA *(she/her)* is a cofounder of Black Lives Matter, the organizing project that challenged the world to combat anti-Black state-sanctioned violence. A lifelong organizer, she also leads Black Futures Lab, which seeks to build Black political power.

ROXANE GAY *(she/her)* is a contributing opinion writer for the *New York Times*. She has written several conversation-stirring books, including *Bad Feminist*, *Difficult Women*, and *Hunger*. She uses her *World of Wakanda* comic series to encourage readers to reimagine the world.

TOM B. K. GOLDTOOTH *(he/him)* is director of Indigenous Environmental Network. Of Diné and Dakota heritage, he is a policy adviser to Indigenous communities on environmental protection. He cofounded the Durban Group for Climate Justice, Climate Justice NOW!, and the US-based Environmental Justice Climate Change initiative.

WINONA GUO *(she/her)* is, with **PRIYA VULCHI**, the cofounder of racial literacy nonprofit CHOOSE and coauthor of *Tell Me Who You Are: Sharing Our Stories of Race, Culture, and Identity*.

DEB HAALAND *(she/her)* was elected as one of the first Native American women (Pueblo of Laguna and Jemez Pueblo) to serve in the United States Congress in the 2016 election. A consistently progressive voice, she represents New Mexico in the House of Representatives.

FRED HAMPTON *(he/him)* was an activist with the Black Panther Party for Self-Defense. He was killed in a joint law enforcement raid on Black Panther Headquarters in Chicago. December 4 has been designated Fred Hampton Day in his native Chicago.

ERIN HEANEY *(she/her)* is director of SURJ: Showing Up for Racial Justice, a national network "working to undermine White supremacy and work toward racial justice."

ASH-LEE WOODARD HENDERSON *(she/her)* bills herself as an Affrilachian (Black Appalachian). A long-time activist, she is the first Black woman to serve as coexecutive director of Highlander Research and Education Center.

RABBI ABRAHAM JOSHUA HESCHEL *(he/him)* was a rabbi, scholar, and educator. He immersed himself in civil rights and anti-war activism and was a professor of Jewish ethics and mysticism at the Jewish Theological Seminary of America.

BELL HOOKS *(she/her)*, born Gloria Jean Watkins, is a scholar who has written dozens of iconic books, from *Ain't I a Woman: Black Women and Feminism* to the children's book *Happy to Be Nappy*. Her work is foundational in Black feminist theory.

ZORA NEALE HURSTON *(she/her)* was an iconic writer and anthropologist of the Harlem Renaissance. She grew up in Eatonville, Florida, and moved to Harlem as a young adult—two settings that influenced much of her literary work.

NOEL IGNATIEV *(he/him)* went from being a steelworker to an historian and author of *How the Irish Became White*, which examines the construction of Whiteness. He also created *Race Traitor*, a journal with the motto: "Treason to Whiteness is loyalty to humanity."

DEEPA IYER *(she/her)* is a writer, attorney, and racial justice advocate. She is the author of *We Too Sing America: South Asian, Arab, Muslim and Sikh Immigrants Shape Our Multiracial Future*, and served as executive director at South Asian Americans Leading Together.

OTIS S. JOHNSON *(he/him)* was the second Black man to serve as mayor of Savannah, Georgia.

SOYA JUNG *(she/her)* is a fixture in the progressive movement. She was executive director of the Washington Alliance for Immigrant and Refugee Justice, founding chair of the Asian and Pacific Islander Coalition, and is senior partner at ChangeLab, which she created to address demographic change and Asian American racial politics.

IBRAM X. KENDI *(he/him)* is founding director of the Antiracist Research and Policy Center at American University and author of *Stamped from the Beginning: The Definitive History of Racist Ideas in America* and *How to Be an Antiracist*. He describes himself as "a hardcore humanist and softcore vegan."

REV. DR. MARTIN LUTHER KING JR.
(he/him) was a driving force of the Civil Rights Movement. He led the Southern Christian Leadership Conference and delivered speeches around the United States that lifted up the idea of using nonviolence to fight violent racism. His most famous speech was 1963's "I Have a Dream," which was delivered on the steps of the Lincoln Memorial in Washington, DC. When he was awarded the Nobel Peace Prize in 1964, he was the youngest man to receive the honor.

RUTH KING *(she/her)* is a life coach and teacher in the Insight Meditation community. A native Californian, she is the author of *Mindful of Race: Transforming Racism from The Inside Out*.

YURI KOCHIYAMA *(she/her)* was a social justice and human rights activist. The daughter of Japanese immigrants, she spent two years living in an internment camp during World War II; it was an experience that shaped the rest of her life. She went on to create Asian Americans for Action and worked to link the political struggles of Asian and Black Americans.

HARI KONDABOLU *(he/him)* is a comedian, podcaster, and activist. He holds a master's degree in human rights from the London School of Economics. The *New York Times* describes him as "one of the most exciting political comics in stand-up today." His documentary *The Problem with Apu* called out *The Simpsons* for its racist characterization of one of the show's few characters of color.

KIYOSHI KUROMIYA *(he/him)* was a third-generation Japanese American civil-rights and gay-rights activist. Born in a concentration camp at Hart Mountain, he was an integral part of several movements, cofounding the Gay Liberation Front and embedding himself within the Black Power Movement.

KIESE LAYMON *(he/him)* is a Black, southern, award-winning writer who was born and raised in Jackson, Mississippi. His latest book, *Heavy: An American Memoir*, was named one of the best books of 2018 by multiple media outlets.

LECRAE *(he/him)* is a Grammy Award-winning hip-hop artist whose music centers his faith in Jesus and his care for people typically pushed to the margins. He is the author of *Unashamed*.

QUEEN LILI'UOKALANI *(she/her)* was the last ruler of Hawai'i's Kal'kaua dynasty. She was a major advocate for a sovereign nation, and she was pushed off the throne via a coup d'état led by colonizers (and backed by the United States military).

ZACK LINLY *(he/him)* is an Atlanta-based activist and poet.

LIZZO *(she/her)* is a chart-topping, Grammy Award-winning singer and songwriter whose music centers positivity and self-love.

AUDRE LORDE *(she/her)* was a celebrated writer, activist, and educator. A foundational Black feminist, her work spoke to the fight for liberation for people who are oppressed because of their race, gender, sexuality, and class. She was an early advocate of the idea—the fact—that there can be no freedom for one if there is no freedom for all.

MIRIAM MAKEBA *(she/her)* was a singular singer and vocal figure in the anti-apartheid movement.

NELSON MANDELA *(he/him)* was South Africa's first Black president and its first democratically elected leader. His journey to leadership took him through transformative work with the African National Congress, charges of treason, twenty-seven years in prison, and a successful battle to end the discriminatory practice of apartheid. He was awarded the Nobel Peace Prize for his unwavering commitment to liberation.

BECKIE MASAKI *(she/her)* is social justice and community building director at the Asian Pacific Institute on Gender-Based Violence. Her identities of survivor and immigrant inform her approach to grassroots activism.

PASTOR MICHAEL McBRIDE *(he/him)* is a national faith leader committed to leading a holistic ministry that trains and supports millennials and religious institutions tackling racial justice and Black liberation. A graduate of Duke University's Divinity School, he leads The Way Christian Center in West Berkeley, California, and serves as director of Faith in Action's Live Free Campaign.

SHANE McCRAE *(he/him)* is a poet who lives in New York City and teaches at Columbia University. He has written many books, including *In the Language of My Captor* and *Sometimes I Never Suffered*.

MATT McGORRY *(he/him)* is an actor, activist, and intersectional feminist who works to make his fellow White people recognize and properly use their privilege.

REV. DR. BRENDA SALTER McNEIL *(she/her)* is an ordained pastor in the Evangelical Covenant Church and director of the Reconciliation Studies program at Seattle Pacific University.

JONATHAN METZL *(he/him)* is a psychiatrist and director of the Center for Medicine, Health, and Society at Vanderbilt University. Author of *Dying of Whiteness: How the Politics of Racial Resentment Is*

Killing America's Heartland, his work connects the dots—and chasms—between gun violence, race, and mental illness in America.

CINDY MILSTEIN *(she/her)* is an author and anarchist whose advocacy drives her to work with collectives that center the creation of autonomous spaces of resistance, education, and reconstruction.

DARNELL MOORE *(he/him)* has been called "one of the most influential Black writers and thinkers of our time." He studied at Princeton Theological Seminary and is author of *No Ashes in the Fire: Coming of Age Black and Free in America*; he uses his voice to save the lives of people pushed to the edges of society.

TONI MORRISON *(she/her)* was an iconic author whose work offered Black people in America a glimpse of themselves on a page. She was awarded the Pulitzer Prize and the National Book Critics Circle Award, and she was the first Black woman to win the Nobel Prize in Literature.

JESSE A. MYERSON *(he/him)* is a community organizer with volunteer political operation Hoosier Action in Bloomington, Indiana.

HUEY P. NEWTON *(he/him)* cofounded the Black Panther Party for Self Defense in Oakland, California, in 1966. As the organization's minister of defense, he advocated for the dismantling of a system built to subjugate Black people in America.

BARACK OBAMA *(he/him)* served as the forty-fourth president of the United States. He was the first Black person to hold that office.

ALEXANDRIA OCASIO-CORTEZ *(she/her)* is an educator and organizer who serves the Bronx as a member of the United States House of Representatives. She is committed to social, racial, economic, and environmental justice advocacy.

JONA OLSSON *(she/her)* is the New Mexico-based activist and educator who founded cultural bridges to justice, which provides cultural diversity training for nonprofits.

IJEOMA OLUO *(she/her)* is a writer and self-proclaimed "internet yeller." She is the author of the *New York Times* bestseller *So You Want to Talk About Race*, and she was named one of *The Root's* Most Influential African Americans in 2017.

POPE PAUL VI *(he/him)*—born Giovanni Battista Montini—was head of the Catholic church. He was made a saint in 2018.

LEONARD PELTIER *(he/him)* advocates for the rights of Indigenous people via his work with the American Indian Movement and other organizations. He is a member of the Anishinaabe, Dakota, and Lakota Nations, and has been in prison for three decades, convicted of killing two FBI agents during a 1975 shoot-out on the Pine Ridge Indian Reservation. He—and millions of supporters—maintain his innocence.

ELLEN PENCE *(she/her)* was cofounder of the Duluth Domestic Abuse Intervention Project and director of Praxis International, and she pioneered a collaborative model for supporting victims of intimate partner violence that is used worldwide. She also advocated for reform to address racial disparity in the child welfare system.

IMANI PERRY *(she/her)* is the Hughes-Rogers Professor of African American Studies at Princeton University. A prolific author, the Birmingham, Alabama-born scholar's books include *Breathe: A Letter to My Sons*.

JODI PICOULT *(she/her)* is an award-winning novelist with more than two dozen books in print.

ELLEN POMPEO *(she/her)* is an actress, producer, and director best known for leading the cast of the long-running television show *Grey's Anatomy*.

FRANCHESCA RAMSEY *(she/her)* is a writer, actress, and producer who first went viral with her online video "Shit White Girls Say . . . to Black Girls." Her video projects—like her MTV web series *Decoded*—frequently break down seemingly complex race-related topics and make them easy for all to understand.

PATRICIA G. RAMSEY *(she/her)* is an early childhood anti-bias educator for both children and the adults who loom large in their lives. She cowrote *What If All the Kids Are White?: Anti-Bias Multicultural Education with Young Children and Families* with **LOUISE DERMAN-SPARKS**.

MEGAN RAPINOE *(she/her)* is cocaptain of the US Women's National Soccer Team and an advocate for LGBTQIA+ rights and racial equality. To call her outspoken is to master the understatement; she was one of the first athletes to kneel in solidarity with Colin Kaepernick's campaign to draw attention to police violence.

JASON REYNOLDS *(he/him)* writes poetry and novels for young adult and middle-grade audiences; he is a National Book Award Finalist for Young People's Literature and the *New York Times*-bestselling author of *Miles Morales: Spider-Man*, the Track series, and *Long Way Down*.

BAYARD RUSTIN *(he/him)* was a key adviser to Martin Luther King Jr., and the brilliant mind who pulled together the 1963 March on Washington for Jobs and Freedom. He was openly gay and passionately advocated for civil rights for queer people of color.

BUFFY SAINTE-MARIE *(she/her)* is a singer-songwriter. The Canada-reared Cree activist is the first Indigenous person to win an Academy Award—for cowriting the song "Up Where We Belong"—and the first woman to breastfeed on national television (on *Sesame Street*!).

ARTURO ALFONSO SCHOMBURG *(he/him)* is the Schomburg Center for Research in Black Culture's namesake. The Black, Puerto Rico-born scholar and lover of the written word cofounded the Negro Society for Historical Research and archived books and other written materials created by Black people across the Americas and Europe.

SARAH SHIN *(she/her)* serves as associate national director of evangelism for InterVarsity Christian Fellowship. A painter and public speaker, she also provides trainings that bring together the topics of ethnicity, evangelism, and the arts.

BELLAMY SHOFFNER *(she/her)* is creator of *Hold the Line*, a magazine that explores the intersection of social justice and parenting.

LEANNE BETASAMOSAKE SIMPSON *(she/her)* is an award-winning Michi Saagiig Nishnaabeg writer, musician, and educator. She is the author of many books, including *Dancing on Our Turtle's Back: Stories of Nishnaabeg Re-Creation, Resurgence, and a New Emergence*, and has lectured at universities across Canada.

SONIA SOTOMAYOR *(she/her)* is an associate justice on the United States Supreme Court. Nominated by President Barack Obama, the Yale Law School-educated Puerto Rican powerhouse is the nation's first Latinx justice.

AMANDLA STENBERG *(they/them, she/her)* is an actress and activist who uses their platform to advocate for Black people and people in the LGBTQIA+ community.

BRYAN STEVENSON *(he/him)* is the founder and executive director of Equal Justice Initiative, a human rights organization based in Montgomery, Alabama. He led the effort to create the National Memorial for Peace and Justice and has dedicated his legal career to challenging abuses in the United States' carceral system.

DERALD WING SUE *(he/him)* is a professor of psychology at Teachers College, Columbia University, and cofounder of the Asian American Psychological Association. He is author of several books, including *Race Talk and the Conspiracy of Silence: Understanding and Facilitating Difficult Dialogues on Race*.

DR. BEVERLY DANIEL TATUM *(she/her)* is the former president of Spelman College and the author of *Why Are All the Black Kids Sitting Together in the Cafeteria? And Other Conversations About Race*.

HENRY DAVID THOREAU *(he/him)* was a writer, abolitionist, and educator. A Transcendentalism devotee, he is best known for his philosophical writings, including *Walden*.

JEMAR TISBY *(he/him)* is president of The Witness, a Black Christian collective, host of the *Pass the Mic* podcast, and author of *The Color of Compromise: The Truth About the American Church's Complicity in Racism*.

OPAL TOMETI *(she/her)* is a human rights advocate, strategist, and writer. She is also one of the brilliant minds behind Black Lives Matter. She served as executive director of Black Alliance for Just Immigration and was a Frederick Douglass 200 awardee for her contributions to contemporary social movements.

KYLE "GUANTE" TRAN MYHRE *(he/him)* is a poet, educator, and activist. His work explores identity, power, and resistance. A two-time National Poetry Slam champion, he uses poetry as a jumping-off point for community building.

SOJOURNER TRUTH *(she/her)* escaped slavery, found her calling as a preacher, and used her ability to command a crowd to advocate for abolition and women's rights via enduring speeches like, "Ain't I a Woman?" She also worked with the Freedmen's Bureau, helping the formerly enslaved build new, free lives.

RIGOBERTA MENCHÚ TUM *(she/her)* is a K'iche' activist and organizer born in Guatemala. She was awarded the Nobel Peace Prize in 1992 for her work around ethnocultural reconciliation and the expansion of rights for Indigenous people around the word.

ARCHBISHOP DESMOND TUTU *(he/his)* was the first Black general secretary of the South African Council of Churches, who took as his mission the creation of "a democratic and just society without racial divisions." He won the Nobel Peace Prize in 1984 for his work opposing apartheid in South Africa.

JONATHAN VAN NESS *(he/him)* is a genderqueer nonbinary activist and lover of all things ice skating. He is one of the hosts on Netflix's *Queer Eye*, has a podcast called *Getting Curious with Jonathan Van Ness*, and is author of the *New York Times*-bestselling book *Over the Top: A Raw Journey to Self Love*.

PRIYA VULCHI *(she/her)* is, with **WINONA GUO**, the cofounder of racial literacy nonprofit CHOOSE and coauthor of *Tell Me Who You Are: Sharing Our Stories of Race, Culture, and Identity*.

NAYYIRAH WAHEED *(she/her)* is a poet and author of the books *salt.* and *nejma*.

WAZIYATAWIN *(she/her)* is a Wahpetunwan Dakota educator and activist from the Pezihutazizi Otunwe (Yellow Medicine Village) in what is now called Minnesota. She is the Indigenous Peoples Research Chair at University of Victoria and her research centers decolonization, resistance, and liberation strategies.

IDA B. WELLS *(she/her)* was an educator and journalist who put her life in great peril to investigate the lynchings of Black men. She challenged White women to draw connections between their oppressors and those of Black people, and she founded the National Association of Colored Women's Club, which fought for civil rights and suffrage for *all* women.

ELAINE WELTEROTH *(she/her)* is a journalist, author, and television personality. She became the youngest person ever to serve as editor-in-chief of a major magazine when she took over at *Teen Vogue* and was the first Black judge on *Project Runway*.

SERENA WILLIAMS *(she/her)* is unequivocally one of the best athletes of all time across all sports. She—and sister Venus—began playing tennis professionally in 1995 and she has dominated the game for decades. Williams never misses a chance to speak out about injustice as she pushes through in a world that seeks to vilify her for being confident and assertive.

SCOTT WOODS *(he/him)* is a Columbus, Ohio-based writer. Author of *Urban Contemporary History Month*, he also cofounded Writers' Block Poetry Night and served as president of Poetry Slam, Inc.

MALCOLM X *(he/him)*, also known as el-Hajj Malik el-Shabazz, was an American activist who was one of the most influential leaders of the Civil Rights Movement and the Nation of Islam. He was assassinated in 1965, but his stature only grew, particularly after the publication of his bestselling book, *The Autobiography of Malcolm X*. Written with journalist Alex Haley, it's a classic that continues to influence readers today.

HELEN ZIA *(she/her)* is an activist and author. A Fulbright Scholar and the daughter of immigrants from China, she advocates for women's rights and works to counter hate, violence, and homophobia.

PHOTO CREDITS

P. 10: Alicia Garza: Reproduced by permission of Kristin Little, KristinLittle.com.

P. 13: Franchesca Ramsey: Reproduced by permission of Joey Islandboi Rosado.

PP. 16–17: Barack Obama: © Shutterstock.com/mistydawnphoto.

P. 20: Archbishop Desmond Tutu: © Shutterstock.com/Lorna Roberts.

P. 23: Alexandria Ocasio-Cortez: © Shutterstock.com/Jstone.

P. 30: Opal Tometi: Reproduced by permission of O'Shea Tometi.

P. 32: Malcolm X: Hiller, Herman. *Malcolm X at Queens Court / World Telegram & Sun photo by Herman Hiller.* Black and white photograph, 1964. Library of Congress: loc.gov/item/97519439/.

P. 35: Anna Julia Cooper: Bell, C. M. *Mrs. A. J. Cooper.* Black and white photograph, ca. 1901–1903. Library of Congress: loc.gov/item/2016702852/.

PP. 38–39: Buffy Sainte-Marie: © Dreamstime.com/Cameron Hughes. ID 97105776.

P. 41: Dennis Banks: © CSU Archives/Everett Collection. Stock.Adobe.com.

P. 45: Frantz Fanon: © CSU Archives/Everett Collection. Stock.Adobe.com.

P. 46: Ida B. Wells: Cihak and Zima. *Wells-Barnett, Ida B.* Black and white photograph, 1893–1894. University of Chicago Photographic Archive, [apf108637], Special Collections Research Center, University of Chicago Library.

P. 51: César Chávez: Trikosko, Marion S. *Interview with Cesar Chavez. 4/20/1979. Chavez gesturing.* Black and white photograph, 1979. Library of Congress: loc.gov/item/2016646413/.

PP. 52–53: Bayard Rustin: Wolfson, Stanley. *Bayard Rustin, half-length portrait, facing front, microphones in foreground / World Telegram & Sun photo by Stanley Wolfson.* Black and white photograph, 1965. Library of Congress: loc.gov/item/97518846/.

P. 57: Lizzo: © Dreamstime.com/Featureflash. ID 165599481.

P. 59: Darnell Moore. Reproduced by permission of Paul Stewart Jr.

P. 62: Laverne Cox: © Shutterstock.com/Kathy Hutchins.

PP. 64–65: Deb Haaland: Reproduced by permission of Deb for Congress.

P. 68: Henry David Thoreau: Parlow, Geo F. *Henry David Thoreau, head-and-shoulders portrait, facing slightly right.* Black and white photograph, 1879. Library of Congress: loc.gov/item/95513963/.

P. 71: James Baldwin: Van Vechten, Carl. *Portrait of James Baldwin.* Black and white photograph, 1955. Library of Congress: loc.gov/item/2004662552/.

P. 74: Sojourner Truth: *Sojourner Truth. I sell the shadow to support the substance.* Black and white photograph, 1864. Library of Congress, Rare Book and Special Collections Division, Alfred Whital Stern Collection of Lincolniana. Loc.gov/item/scsm000880/.

P. 76: Kiyoshi Kuromiya: Philadelphia FIGHT. *Staff of the Philadelphia AIDS Library.* Black and White photograph, date unknown. http://outhistory.org/exhibits/show/philadelphia-lgbt-interviews/interviews/kiyoshi-kuromiya.

PP. 80–81: Bryan Stevenson: Reproduced by permission of Equal Justice Initiative.

P. 84: Elaine Welteroth: © Shutterstock/Udo Salters Photography.

P. 87: Frederick Douglass: Conly, C. F, and G. K. Warren. *Frederick Douglass / C. F. Conly Photographer, 465 Washington St., Boston.* Black and white photograph, ca. 1800–1890. Library of Congress: loc.gov/item/2018651422/.

PP. 90–91: Megan Rapinoe: © Shutterstock.com/Jose Breton—Pics Action.

P. 94: Marian Anderson: Van Vechten, Carl. *Portrait of Marian Anderson singing.* Black and white photograph, 1940. Library of Congress: loc.gov/item/2004662513/.

P. 96: Ruth King: Reproduced by permission of Vaschelle André, Divine Photography.

PP. 100–101: Miriam Makeba: © Reuters/Claudia Daut. Stock.Adobe.com.

P. 106: Leanne Betasamosake Simpson: Reproduced by permission of Nadya Kwandibens, Red Works Photography.

P. 111: Nelson Mandela, Keating, Maureen. *President of South Africa, Nelson Mandela with members of the Congressional Black Caucus including Representative Kweisi Mfume, at an event at the Library of Congress*. Black and white photograph, 1994. Library of Congress: loc.gov/item/2015645189/.

P. 114: Sonia Sotomayor: © Reuters/Dominick Reuter. Stock.Adobe.com

P. 117: Queen Lili'uokalani: *Lili'uokalani, Queen of Hawaii, full-length portrait, seated, outdoors, with dog, facing slightly left*. Black and white photograph, 1917. Library of Congress: loc.gov /item/92513983/.

P. 120: Lecrae: © Reuters/Danny Moloshok. Stock .Adobe.com.

P. 125: Susan B. Anthony: Johnson, Frances Benjamin. *Susan B. Anthony*. Black and white photograph, ca. 1915–1920. Library of Congress: loc.gov/item/2014710283/.

PP. 126–127: Serena Williams: © Shutterstock.com/ Lev Radin.

P. 131: Shawn Dove: Reproduced by permission of Tamara Fleming, Tamara Fleming Photography.

P. 133: W. Kamau Bell: Reproduced by permission of John Nowak, CNN/WarnerMedia.

P. 136: Ozy Aloziem: Reproduced by permission of Ozy Aloziem.

P. 138: Zora Neale Hurston: Van Vechten, Carl. *Portrait of Zora Neale Hurston*. Black and white photograph, 1938. Library of Congress: loc .gov /item/2004663047/.

P. 143: Wazíyatawin: Reproduced by permission of the Wilson Family.

P. 145: Toni Morrison: © Dreamstime.com/Olga Besnard. ID 9915227.

ACKNOWLEDGMENTS

Thanks to my publisher, Sharyn Rosart, for being a joy to work with and for trusting me to advance her vision for a new imprint that centers personal integrity and emotional intelligence. *insert air horn* And to designer Lynne Yeamans, photo researcher Jennifer Rudsit, and copyeditor Jill Saginario for making our little book sing. Shout out to my literary agent team, Tanya McKinnon and Carol Taylor, for making shit happen. Big love to Bola Williams for the support and celebrations. Thank you to Erica Easter and Ayana Byrd for the constant encouragement. And my entire heart to my little, Saa Rankin Naasel, for giving me hope.

Printed in Canada

SPRUCE BOOKS with colophon is a registered trademark of Penguin Random House LLC

24 23 22 21 20   9 8 7 6 5 4 3 2 1

Editor: Sharyn Rosart | Designer: Lynne Yeamans | Cover designer: Lynne Yeamans and Alicia Terry

Library of Congress Cataloging-in-Publication Data is available.

Grateful acknowledgment is made to the following:
Page 76: Kiyoshi Kuromiya, interviewed by Marc Stein, June 17, 1997. For the audiotape, see John J. Wilcox, Jr. Archives, William Way LGBT Community Center. For a transcript, see http://outhistory.org/exhibits/show/philadelphia-lgbt-interviews/interviews/kiyoshi-kuromiya. Reprinted by permission.
Page 136: Courtesy of Ozy Aloziem. Twitter. https://twitter.com/arisyre/status/1195403554720305155. Reprinted by permission by the author.
Page 141: Shane McCrae. "Jim Limber's Theodicy," *Sometimes I Never Suffered*. New York: Farrar, Straus and Giroux, 2020. Reprinted by permission by the author.

FOR A FULL LIST OF CITATIONS FOR EACH QUOTE APPEARING IN THIS BOOK, PLEASE VISIT KENRYA.COM.

ISBN: 978-1-63217-340-9

Spruce Books, a Sasquatch Books Imprint
1904 Third Avenue, Suite 710, Seattle, WA 98101

SasquatchBooks.com

KENRYA RANKIN is an award-winning author, journalist, and editorial consultant whose insight has been tapped by leading outlets, including the *New York Times*, the *Huffington Post*, and ThinkProgress. She creates dynamic content that amplifies the lived experiences, advocacy, and work of people of color and shifts the narrative around who deserves liberation, justice, and dignity in America. A twenty-year veteran in the editorial space, she is also cohost of *The Turn On* podcast, principal at Perfectly Said Studio, and the author of five books, including *How We Fight White Supremacy: A Field Guide to Black Resistance*. As a journalist and editor, her work has appeared in dozens of national publications, including *Reader's Digest, Ebony, Fast Company,* and *Redbook,* and has been translated into twenty-one languages. The Cleveland native is a graduate of Howard University and New York University. When she's not working, she enjoys baking and having Beyoncé dance parties with her brilliant daughter.